terrible, violent, (beautiful)

Jess Thompson

Presentation by *BookLeaf Publishing*

Web: www.bookleafpub.com

E-mail: info@bookleafpub.com

ISBN: 978-93-5744-392-0

First edition 2022

DEDICATION

Dedicated to my grandmother, who endured years and years of me begging her to read to me.

You brought magic into my life through books. I'll never be able to repay you for that.

ACKNOWLEDGEMENT

I hold constant gratitude for my parents for always supporting my writing endeavors and everything else that I do. They have never once made me feel incapable of achieving any and all of my ambitions, and that sort of unwavering belief is unrepayable.

A huge acknowledgement to Kate Walters, my best friend and my one-woman editing army, who dealt with some truly obscure first drafts and tore my poems apart to create the best versions of themselves, while also leaving encouraging comments such as, "throwing up over this one. but affectionately." Couldn't do it without you and frankly, wouldn't have wanted to.

And as always, with every strong writer is an English teacher who believed in them when it mattered the most. Melissa - thank you for curating my love of writing at a young age, even though I constantly refused to read any of it in front of the class. I'm sorry for being such a menace with terrible handwriting. But hey look! At least now I'm a menace with terrible handwriting AND a published book of poems!

PREFACE

And I seem to have such strength in me now, that I think I could stand anything, any suffering, only to be able to say and to repeat to myself every moment, "I exist." In thousands of agonies - I exist. I'm tormented on the rack - but I exist! Though I sit alone in a pillar - I exist! I see the sun, and if I don't see the sun, I know it's there.

And there's a whole life in that, in knowing that the sun is there.

- Fyodor Dostoevsky

An Introduction

Hello.

I'd like to introduce myself.

I am

> a friend
> *(it would do you well not to trust me)*

> a writer
> *(a professional liar)*

and a poet.
(all i do is think and think and think and sometimes i feel something and sometimes it gets written down)

It's lovely to meet you.

Violent Tendencies

There's a certain fascination in the cycle of
beauty and violence.

That is not to say that one cannot exist without
the other,
But rather to say that art can be both
         facilitated by
and also
         an answer to.

I have never once considered my violent
tendencies beautiful.

The scars I wear are not romantic.
         They are desperate mistakes drug across
porcelain skin.
But art whispers that they are instead reminders
of an internal war that I have won over and over
and over again. Art whispers, *look. You are
undefeated.*

The blood that I bleed is not beautiful.
         It is dark and heavy and sticky and red.

But art whispers that it is instead the ichor of
gods, the proof of my humanity. Art whispers,
look. You are made of stardust.

I don't know if there's a correct answer

(I don't know if I want a correct answer)

But I do think that there is a morbid fascination
in continuing
to live
            struggle
                    fight
for the terrible
                    violent
                            (beautiful)
anyway.

Detachment

The sun was setting when we left the station
It'll take 2 hours and 31 minutes to get home
I like watching the lights come into focus as we
slow and stop at a station
(There are 8 more stops to go)
I like watching the lights then blur as we pick up
speed again
I read somewhere that trains can reach up to 220
miles per hour
I wonder how fast we're moving now.
It doesn't feel right to say that this train is taking
me home
But at the moment, I don't have another word.
I'll think about it.
My home used to be a little city of 168,302
people
But then I moved 4,907 miles away and it
become a little city of 168,301
And that's no longer my home either.
Tonight is the first snow of the season and I can
sometimes see the flurries through the window,
But mostly I just see my reflection
And the occasional light or two from a home in
the English countryside

- the night train home from london

Smile

She had never considered the color of horror until she found herself trapped in that terrible cream room surrounded by terrible pale men in terrible white lab coats.

She had never considered herself feral until they shoved sharpened hooks into the meat of her cheeks as she shrieked in pain and desperately tried to bite disgusting prodding fingers.

"We just want to see that beautiful smile of yours," they told her. She watched the blood drip from her face onto her thighs.

"Can't you just give us a smile? Last chance, sweetie," they tried again. She spit on the ground and dejected sighs filled the terrible room.

The machine whirred as it turned on and the hooks tightened in her flesh and applause broke out across the room as the bloody skewered meat of her cheeks were lifted to the sky to reveal a gruesome grin.

"See?" they said. "You look so beautiful when you smile."

She had never considered true hatred until she tasted the salt of her tears falling into the decadent display of her forged smile.

love as an academic

- analogizing workings in math with rhythms in poetry, comparing nikola tesla and edgar allan poe
- honey covered compliments in greek and latin and german and *i will resurrect a dead language if it will finally give me enough words to tell you how fiercely i love you*
- slow dancing in the living room to tchaikovsky, careful not to bump the chessboard less we interrupt the pieces of the abandoned game
- handwritten notes slipped into textbooks and gentle kisses on fingers smudged with ink
- nicknames referencing niche and unknown poets & scientists & authors & painters, calling you donatello because you are nothing if not an idealist
- the uncanny ability to sense the burn out spiral approaching and applying a grounding weight through hands on shoulders and in hair
- whispers of *it's okay* and *you're doing great* and *take a deep breath* and coming out of the spiral and realizing it's 4am and oh god it's 4am?

- and they smile at you when you resurface and
with bags under their eyes and exhaustion
weighing on their limbs still they offer you all
their fondness when they whisper, *there you are.
welcome back, my love.*

Recognizable

The clouds here are different.
They gather lower in the sky as they discuss the
comings and goings of their day.
Hi, I call out.
> *You shouldn't be here*, they tell me.
But I am here. I live here now.
> *Hmm.*
There's something lonely about how the clouds
don't recognize me anymore.
Perhaps the wind will.
I'll try again tomorrow.

A Quick Guide to Being Brought Back from the Dead

1. Let me be the first to welcome you back. Are you cold? You must be cold. Let me get you a blanket.
2. Take a drink of water - it'll wash the dirt out of your throat. If you pour some in your hands and splash it on your face, it should help the itching in your eyes.
3. Hey, quick question - did you meet God? You don't have to answer, I suppose that's rude to ask.
4. You're going to be nauseous for a while. You were, after all, dead. You're bound to feel some vertigo upon returning.
5. Are you still cold? I'll grab more blankets.
6. Walking is going to be hard. You don't have any muscle - you're going to have to build it up all over again. Don't worry, I brought a wheelchair to get you out of here. We can schedule physical therapy tomorrow.
7. Your funeral was lovely, but don't ask about details. It'll just hurt your head.
8. In fact, maybe don't ask any questions about how you died. It's best if you don't know.
9. Do you still like chocolate?

Divinity

Van Gogh wanted to be a preacher before he
became a painter
He saw divinity in this world
And he so badly wanted to understand.
He took a paintbrush to a canvas and carved his
pain
And begged his gods to answer
Look, his paintings said. *Look. I am here.*
Do you see me?
And while Van Gogh's artistic career was short
compared to most,
There is something so beautiful in dedicating a
decade of his life
To a search for divinity in the only way he
could.
I sometimes wonder if he ever got a reply.

Fear Response

In 8th grade, I learned that fear is an
evolutionary trait
And that those without it would not survive.
Death is, after all, a knife with which evolution
delicately carves her children
And the most effective monsters mimic our
ancestral horrors.

With this in mind, it is intriguing to consider the
uncanny valley effect.
The identifiable fact that something is like ones
self
But it is also not.
And this unsettles us.
Something is missing, our brains tell us in urgent
nerve firings.

Something is wrong.

It is argued that this immediate response of
repulse is due to what is horribly different
But I'd like to counter that it is instead due to
what is horribly the same.

After all,

When I see someone who looks like you,
My chest freezes and my brain screams at me to
run
  oh god
     RUN
And this is not because I rationally know that it
isn't you
But because for a brief moment,
I feared it was.

to be great does not necessarily mean to be good

John Steinbeck wrote, "And now that you don't
have to be perfect, you can be good."
And that's just it, isn't it?
I'm not sure I know how to be good.
I know how to do perfect
I can scratch and claw and fight my way to
perfect
And with blood under my nails and a smile that
looks too close to dangerous
I can claim greatness
I'm not sure I can ever claim goodness
As a being with a potentially terrible soul
Edgar Allan Poe wrote, "Tell me every terrible
thing you ever did, and let me love you
anyway."

> *- a poem in which can be read forward
> or backward*

to-do list

to do: wake up
to do: turn on the coffee machine
to do: linger, wander, watch the neighborhood
cats out the window
to do: pour yourself a cup once the coffee is
properly heated
to do: add milk to the grocery list
to do: maybe today you'll go for a walk
to do: wrap yourself in a blanket and sit by the
heater
to do: email the landlord that the heater broke,
again
to do: try to remember that at one time, you had
hobbies
to do: what were your hobbies?
to do: they must not have been very important
to do: read a chapter of your new book you were
excited about at some point
to do: get another cup of coffee
to do: it's cold now
to do: didn't you have something important to do
today?
to do: climb back into bed
to do: maybe tomorrow will be easier
to do: resolve to try again tomorrow

An Exceptional Day

It's an exceptional day in the underworld
Because the Grim Reaper does not feel like
going to work.
Normally he doesn't mind
But today is an exception.

Today the winds are gentle
And the air smells of pomegranates
And it is like every other day except

He is tired

And the Grim Reaper simply does not feel like
being Death today.
Can the world not last one day without him?
He deserves a break, after all.
So today life will carry on
Because the Grim Reaper will not knock.

And so today is an exception.
An exceptional day.
A day, except

Conversation Etiquette

I found an angel outside a 7/11.
She had six arms and claws in place of fingers
and her face blurred every time I tried to look at
it.
"Don't do that," she told me. "It'll ruin your
eyes."
"Sorry," I replied. "Would you like me to light
that for you?"
She had been holding a cigarette and staring at
an orange lighter that lay on the stained cement
ground.
She nodded and I made sure not to look at her
face again.

I came back the next day and there she stood,
hunched over in front of the dirty little shop.
"Did you get kicked out of heaven?" I asked.
She shrugged. I lit her cigarette and sat on the
cement beside her feet.
We didn't speak for the rest of the day. I said
goodbye with a simple nod and averted eyes.

"I got tired of being holy," she told me a few
days later. "I did something blasphemous."

I nodded solemnly. "One time I stole a salt grinder from Olive Garden."

She took a deep inhale of her cigarette and blew the smoke directly into my face.

"You're not very good at social cues," she informed me.

"I'm not sure what you mean."

"Of course you aren't."

Paralysis of Choice

Søren Kierkegaard: the father of existentialism
and the bane of my existence.

Kierkegaard wrote, "Anxiety is the dizziness of
freedom,"
And dammit, if that didn't ruin my life a little
bit.

When given absolute and undeniable freedom
I suppose I cannot help but panic under the
incomprehensible weight it entails
And instead beg for some sort of safety net in
the form of rules.

If I am indeed free, then shouldn't I be doing
something meaningful and productive and
uplifting and worthy of my capital F Freedom at
every single waking moment?

It's a stifling conundrum that will end with the
majority of my life being focused on
          choosing what to do
rather than
          choosing and doing.

Kierkegaard also wrote, "Do it or do not do it.
You will regret both."

chekhov's gun

some things I know:
sharks don't actually kill that many people per
year
vodka from a plastic bottle tastes better than
disappointment
I always regret the burn of 2am cigarettes come
dawn
I have been alive for 23 years, allegedl

some other things I know:
people love to pick fights
chekhov's gun suggests all details are important
angels don't have heartbeats
tyrannicide is a brilliant word

some things I wish I didn't know:
god created dinosaurs as an experiment to see
what he could do
(he created the asteroid to see what he could
undo)
the feeling of your audacious hands cupping my
jaw
the articulate frenzy of revolution falling from
your lips

sometimes it goes like this:
our blood thrives in the darkness of our bodies
a demon's first day on earth is spent learning
how to breathe
occam's razor tells me that the correct answer is
the simple one
the next sentence I start with "I" will not end in
"love you."

A Family Watches the Apocalypse

I sit on the front porch with my brothers.
One cracks open a beer; the other shoves his
hands in his pockets as the wind plays with his
hair.
We stare at the sky as the stars flare up in
magnificent explosions then dim then fall
One by one.

"Look," my older brother says. "There go the
neighbors."
We watch as suitcases are thrown into a dirty old
pickup
And we watch that pickup peel out of the
driveway and disappear down the road.
I wonder how they plan to escape the
inescapable. We're silent for a long while after
that.

"I thought the end of the world would be more
exciting," my younger brother says.
"I thought there would be more fires," I agree.
"This is exactly what I pictured," my older
brother counters.

Half the stars have gone now.

Our parents join us on the porch.
"Have you seen any angels yet?" my father asks,
cradling a mug of coffee.
He always has an air of tranquility that I've only
ever seen him manage before.
Even on doomsday that truth remains. We shake
our heads.

"I want to know if they're really eight feet tall
with a thousand eyes," my mother says.
"That would be really cool," I agree.
She sits next to me on the steps and holds my
hand, a bottle of tequila loosely gripped in the
other.
The stars continue to fall.

Insomnia

I don't often forget my dreams, which is rather
unfortunate.
Every evening I fight off the pull of heavy
eyelids and tired bones
Because every night I relive your death and
Every morning my throat is raw from screams
that don't make a sound.
And so instead I will lay on my bed and stare at
a ceiling god who listens and does not reply
While my body sobs from lack of sleep and a
circadian ache
And I will futilely hope that tonight, maybe, you
will be okay.

heavy

it is a very serious thing, to be human. to be
alive. to be broken.
to persevere even as we watch our world burn
around us.
there is a certain heaviness to it all.
and the weight gets heavier and our lungs get
weaker and the smoke rises in anger and we
don't know what to do with our poor breaking
hearts.

and the angels arrive too late
crawling towards us with gouged-out eyes and
long broken fingers that look too much like the
talons we have continued to fend off for days on
end.
it will all be alright, they tell us.
but we see their singed halos and smell the
burning feathers where wings once stood
and the weight gets heavier and our tears fall
harder and our hope escapes us strand by strand
and
we are no longer sure.

it is a very serious thing, to be human.

for we are the ones who have to witness it all.
we are the ones who have to carry the world on
our backs and we are the ones who must not
crumble.

we must not crumble.

and the weight gets heavier and we no longer
have tears to cry and still we persevere because
hell, this is our *home*.
and we are broken and we are bent and we are
tired.
we are so tired.
and we are all that is left.

The Fallen

Day One.
The humans screamed when I fell. I could hear
their shrill voices just barely over the wind.
My brother said he saw his entire existence flash
before him during his fall.
I didn't see anything.
I just heard the screams.
Then I felt the crash.
It burned.
It still burns.

Day Three.
I had to find a vessel.
My brother says that our celestial bodies cause
too much harm down here.
I wish he told me how fragile these bodies are. I
made one mistake and broke all its bones.

This is my second vessel now.
I'll take better care of this one.

Day Four.
I miss my wings.

Day Six.

I'm beginning to feel the side effects of what I
am on this Earth.
I'll try to write down the specifics as they come.
For now, my mouth tastes like honey. And
vodka.
I can't seem to get rid of it.

Day Nine.
Is there anything more blessed than watching the
birds sing?

Day Eleven.
My back aches from the wings it once held.
My teeth never feel sharp enough.

Day Thirteen.
I dreamed about turning last night.
It terrifies me how easy it would be.
I could do it.
I could kill a man, even with these dull teeth.
Even without my wings and my claws.
And I could do it well, I think.

I am forgetting myself.

Day Sixteen.
I am so constantly hungry.
Sometimes, I feel as if I am nothing but ache.

Day Nineteen.
My brother is starting to forget his fall.
"Did it hurt?" he asked me.

Yes. My wings decayed. I reached desperately
for the stars to slow me down. My burns still
smolder. I feel the shadow movements of my
seared feathers. It was pain, and I didn't like it.
It is pain.
I wanted to go back.

I want to go back.

Why are my hands shaking?

Day Twenty-One.
My brother no longer remembers who he was
before this life, in this vessel of his.
My brother no longer remembers me.
He fell three days before I did.

Day Twenty-Two.
I am so scared.

Day Twenty-Three.
I can't remember my fall. But I had been
someone before the fall.
Hadn't I?
What was it like to be holy?

I am so scared.

Day Twenty-Four.
I never had a chance to be soft. I hope this new
life will give me one.

I hope this new life will be good.
I hope I will be good.
I hope

hollowed-out corpses

they gave me polished anger and a knife and a
hatred for the weight of this crown.

they gave me cunning smiles and bones whittled
into shivs and
hollowed out corpses that they asked me to turn
into soldiers.
warriors.
gods.

they'll be yours to command, they whispered.
they'll be mine to kill, I heard.

I am twenty-three and leaving
puddles of blood in my wake.

  - ah, but you wear the crown so well.

A Goodbye

Some reminders:
      All art is based on real-life experienced
      events
      And every poem in this collection is an
      entirely truthful retelling.
      I am your friend.

(lies)
(lies)
(lies)

It was lovely to meet you.

www.ingramcontent.com/pod-product-compliance
Lightning Source LLC
LaVergne TN
LVHW041246200726
843507LV00013B/2838